from birth
to 9 years

by Geraldine Taylor

illustrated by Peter Stevenson

Contents

Acknowledgments:

The author would like to thank the editor of this Guide, Marie Birkinshaw, and the designer, Jason Billin, for all their skill and support. Ladybird would also like to thank the parents and children who have helped us with the development of our reading books, and especially Rachel Ufton and Gill Talbot for their help with this Guide.

The publishers acknowledge the use of the following illustrative material: Pages 16, 28, 44, John Birdsall Photography; cover and pages 4, 7, 11, 46, Tim Clark; pages 30, 34, Lorraine Horsley.

A catalogue record for this book is available from the British Library

Published by Ladybird Books Ltd
A subsidiary of the Penguin Group
A Pearson Company

A letter from Geraldine Taylor

Welcome!

It's exciting to present this Guide, especially now.

Children's reading is newsworthy and controversial. So it's good to look at the most important things for us as parents. I'd like to help you to encourage and inspire your child from his earliest days to become a successful reader who really enjoys reading – who's hooked on books!

Lots of babies and children won't conform exactly to the ages and stages in this Guide. The divisions are simply ways to help you to find your starting point.

Warm wishes,

Geraldine Taylor

Geraldine Taylor MA

is a learning and reading specialist, experienced teacher and broadcaster. She has given workshops on children's learning for thousands of parents around the country and takes in-service training for teachers on parent support. She is the author of *Be Your Child's Natural Teacher* (Impact, 1993) in which she describes her own involvement with her son's education.

Geraldine's special interests are the emotional factors affecting children's learning, and the family as learning supporters. Geraldine is also a popular children's author and an award-winning wildlife writer.

Introduction

What is reading?

Educationalists tend to talk about 'reading behaviours' and often tell us that most children start to read between the ages of $2^1/2$ and $4^1/2$. At this stage educationalists look at why picture books are so important for young children and at how we get meaning and story from pictures.

Parents, however, usually take a more specific view. They see reading as the process by which children get meaning from words. Realistically, we can say that the years between $2^1/2$ and $4^1/2$ are those in which we prepare children for reading – **pre-reading**. From the age of $4^1/2$ upwards, children usually begin to make sense of print – **'real' reading**.

Your child is unique

All children progress at different rates and often learn in different ways. Most children learn to read successfully. What is important is that they should feel happy about themselves and their reading and don't feel that you are comparing them with others.

He or she?

I've alternated the use of he and she between the sections of this book. Obviously all the material is relevant to both boys and girls.

How you can help at home

You are your child's most constant inspiration and support from the earliest months and throughout primary school life.

- Show how much you enjoy your own books.
- Find out more about how children learn to read at each stage of reading development.
- Show pleasure in what your child has achieved and try not to hurry each stage.
- Understand some of the drives and emotional factors affecting learning.
- Offer your child a wide choice of reading material.
- Let your child see *you* reading and writing for lots of different purposes, for example, using catalogues and directories.
- If your school-age child is experiencing reading difficulties, your gentle help at home is vital. Find out the best ways to offer this.

This Guide, in combination with the advice of your child's teacher, will help you as your child learns to read.

Q Shouldn't it all be left to the experts?

A Helping your child to learn to read isn't just about skills, it's also about encouragement, understanding and boosting confidence. Remember, YOU are the expert on your child. You know her best, and your support and your own attitude to reading matter most of all.

Ladybird – First choice for reading

Ladybird understands your need for full information and offers a huge variety of books and stories to appeal to every taste and interest.

Look for the *Ladybird – First choice for...* pages at the end of each section in this Guide. Suggestions are given for the most appropriate Ladybird books for you to share with your child at her particular stage of reading development. The books are referred to by their series number (for example, 9522, S9622) and should be obtainable wherever Ladybird books are sold.

Baby & toddler (0–2½ years)

What is your baby doing?

It may seem as though sleeping, feeding and crying are a baby's main occupations – but all babies come with an awesome urge to find things out. New babies start to learn at once. Right from the very first days, babies are looking, listening, feeling.

Communicating Your baby is learning about you, how you communicate with him and how to communicate with you. When he's a few days old, he knows your voice and before he's 8 weeks old, he'll be 'speaking' to you in his own way – a coo, a burble or a croon. He's learning how to get his needs met and about what the world is like around him.

Looking/observing As the months pass, he'll begin to focus on more and more visual detail. He'll be using his senses to give him the information he needs to make sense of our world – his world.

What can babies see?

Developmental research shows us that newborn babies can see about 200 mm away and can recognise differences in size and shape. At first your baby will look for the contrasts between light and dark and respond best to black and white images. By about 2 months he will be able to look at whole patterns, not just the outlines. As his visual skills develop he will be able to see near and far objects, he will respond to highly contrasting colours and be looking for more complex shapes and patterns. It's some time, however, before he can make sense of the pastel shapes and patterns traditionally used on baby products.

Q Is there any point in using books with young babies?

A Yes. We use books with young babies to make their lives more interesting. Books can help to bring liveliness and variety to the way you talk to your baby. He will gradually understand that books are important. In addition, books establish a strong bond between the people who share them. This can start as early as you let it!

Treat your baby's first books as something special to share, rather than as a way into reading. Let your baby play with the pages. This is what he thinks you are doing. Cuddle up close while you look at books and sing rhymes.

Exploring Your baby is very, very curious, reaching out to explore.

Talking He is beginning to make sounds that come closer and closer to speech. It's especially important to make time to talk together because talking is one of the most fundamental life skills. Talking is also the way young children begin to establish who they are. They start to recognise themselves as unique and separate beings.

Listening This is a skill that you can encourage. Have fun making noises, and talk to your baby about the different sounds you hear.

Storing up words Children are building up a mental store of the names for different objects, and these will be amongst the first words they will need for reading.

The value of nursery rhymes

Nursery rhymes are great to share with babies and young children. They boost language development and imagination, and help to foster an early understanding of sequence and story. They're also fun!

Rhymes with actions encourage movement and body control. Beating rhythm promotes an early feeling for number.

Traditional rhymes are part of our literary and childhood heritage and you'll enjoy remembering the ones you liked best. Several nursery rhyme collections are now available on audio cassette.

Bringing nursery rhymes to life

- Sing to your baby and fill your rhymes with funny sound effects and different voices. Songs and rhymes about animals are ideal.
- Explore nursery rhyme collections to learn some new rhymes. If you don't know the tune, say the words in a sing-song style.
- Your baby will love to hear you say and sing rhymes and jingles over and over again. He will respond to being gently rocked and jiggled and will come to anticipate the movements, the tune and the words.

Try this:

Hoddly poddly puddle and fogs.
Cats are to marry the poodle dogs.
Cats in blue jackets and dogs in red hats.
What will become of the mice and the rats?

Then jog your baby on your knee while you sing:

This is the way the ladies ride,
Nim, nim, nim, nim.
This is the way the gentlemen ride,
Trot, trot, trot.
This is the way the huntsmen ride,
A-gallop, a-gallop, a-gallop.
This is the way the farmers ride,
Flipperty, flapperty, FLOP!

How to use picture books with babies

Hold your baby in a comfortable position on your knee, open the book and point to the picture. Tell your baby what the picture is and then focus on a specific detail. Where possible talk about something that includes your baby.

Taken from Ladybird First focus *Faces*

- Choose picture books with big, clear illustrations.
- Pictures of familiar objects are best.
- Rhyming stories are a good way to keep your baby's attention and to encourage listening skills.
- Ask your baby lots of questions. Obviously, he won't yet be able to answer – but he'll get used to hearing the way that questions sound. You can provide the answers as well for now!

Babies and libraries

It's never to early to join a library. So take your baby along to start a lifelong habit. Most libraries have a children's section and a very knowledgeable children's librarian. Lots of libraries run children's story sessions, too.

Variety for older babies and toddlers

Older babies respond to a wide variety of books, and it's fascinating to watch your baby's changing preferences as he gets older. There are lots to choose from.

Photographic books Babies love to look at clear photos of other babies and toddlers doing just what they do and playing with the same sorts of toys. Photos of real animals are also popular. Bring these to life by making the noises!

Taken from Ladybird Look and talk *Baby words*

Textured books Help your baby to explore the sense of touch and to learn how different things feel.

Noisy books These appeal to babies' curiosity about noises and their love of hearing and doing things again.

Novelty books Flaps and pop-ups delight babies and toddlers.

Mobiles, friezes and posters Make your baby's environment more fun.

Books about ME!

Toddlers love to explore and to find out about their world. It's a time of adventure, of walking and talking. It's a ME age and a time of imitation, too.

Look for simple books that focus on the world of young children and their favourite things. These will give you lots of opportunities to talk and introduce new words to your toddler.

This is also the time when early experiences are especially vivid or daunting… going to the doctor, going to the dentist, seeing farm animals. So look for books that help you to talk about, prepare for and relive these experiences. But don't feel you always have to follow your toddler around with a book! There are so many other ways that he will find out about his world.

Learning how a book works

As far as reading is concerned, toddlers are beginning to understand the 'outer workings' of books.

They need to know how a book works before they can begin to learn about letters and words.

To take an example from elsewhere, older toddlers can understand the outer workings of cars – what we use them for, how to get in them, which way the front is, what sound they make, even the idea of driving. But it will be a very long time before they understand mechanics or are allowed to drive a car. In much the same way, children need first to master the outer workings of reading.

Your toddler will be learning:

- how to hold a book.
- how the front of a book is different from the inside.
- that we keep the book still and turn the pages.
- that the pictures are full of interesting things and are the same each time he sees them.
- that a story is exciting to hear.
- that a story in a particular book says the same thing each time.
- that books come with you and your enthusiasm. They mean exciting times together.

Q How do I teach him all these things?

A The good news is that you don't need to make a conscious effort to teach your toddler how a book works. He'll learn this in the happiest way when you simply share storytimes together.

Now we're talking!

Children who enjoy talking often make the most successful start to reading.

- Really listen to what your child tells you. This shows him how important you think it is.
- If he's struggling with words, be patient and let him finish his own sentences.
- Much of what we say to children consists of instructions: *'Quick, put your coat on!' 'Eat up that potato, please.'* It's good to encourage longer, two-way conversations!
- Asking questions about feelings is great to encourage developing expression. *'Do you think that rabbit feels unhappy? What will cheer him up?'*
- Books are an ideal source of ideas when you need help to develop conversations with your child.

Language acquisition

It is estimated that a 6-year old child will know approximately 8,000 root words of English. If that 6-year old knew about 50 words at 18 months, then that child would have learned nearly 8,000 words in $4\frac{1}{2}$ years, or an average of 5 new words per day.

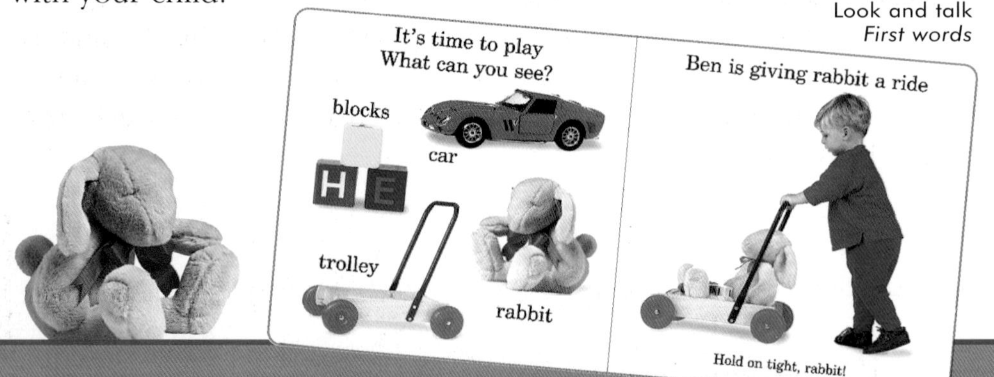

Taken from Ladybird Look and talk *First words*

Repetition

Learning depends on repetition and it's especially important to associate repetition with pleasure. Being close to you, warm and secure, when listening to a story again or singing a rhyme together several times is a strong boost to learning.

Many favourite rhymes and stories for young children contain lots of repetition, of both events and words. Think of *Three Little Pigs*!

It's time for a story!

Enjoying real stories with characters and things that happen is now a natural progression from enjoying early naming and single-sentence books. Try to find time to read stories every day.

- Talk about the story before and afterwards.
- Look at the detail in the pictures. *'Does the King look excited? I wonder what has happened.'*
- Match something in the story to your child's experience and talk about it. *'You were hungry, too, after that long walk.'*
- Vary the time and place you read together. Keep up the bedtime story, too, because this is associated with security, comfort and love.
- Encourage your child to behave like a real reader by holding the book and joining in.
- Novelty and flap books are great to get children involved!

Do it yourselves!

Making things personal and special is very effective for learning. Encourage your toddler to tell you a simple story about his day and to watch while you write his words down. Then read them back to him. This will help him to understand the connection between speech and the written word.

What's the most important thing to remember?

Babies and toddlers are unique and develop at different rates. It's important to really enjoy them as they are and not to hurry each stage along. Look at books together as part of that enjoyment.

First focus

S9318 S939

High contrast black and white books to help your baby to focus his eyes.

Brightly coloured, high contrast books that rattle and squeak.

S935 S936

Touch and feel

Books to appeal to your baby's curiosity about noises and to help him to explore different textures.

S9622

S9621

S9623

Look and talk

Photographic and index tab books to develop your baby's observation and memory skills.

S9514 S9517 S9515

baby and toddler

Picture books

Books that provide lots of opportunities to talk to your baby and introduce new words to your toddler.

944

9510

SL4

Nursery rhymes and storybooks

9435

946*

945*

958

959

947*

9417*

SL1

* Book and tape packs available

Pre-reading ($2\frac{1}{2}$–$4\frac{1}{2}$ years)

What's happening now?

Rapid development continues! Toddlers are becoming young children and will soon be preparing for school. It's a time of excitement, strong emotions, joys and anxieties. One of the most significant periods for learning and memory development occurs between 18 months and 6 years. Children have an increasingly large vocabulary to help them to express their feelings and knowledge.

Books and curiosity

Curiosity is one of the strongest drives in all learning. At first, your child will be curious about why books matter to you, and later, she'll be curious about what happens to the people in a story.

- When you've finished a book, go back and use the story and pictures to ask questions and share possible answers. This will boost imagination and curiosity.
- It isn't always important to come up with the right answer. It's the thinking and wondering that matter, and that children's ideas, feelings and reasoning are taken seriously.

Favourite books!

It's important that your child chooses some of the books when you read together. Your enthusiasm and willingness to read a book frequently will help to make it a favourite. Reading researchers are finding that having a favourite book at age 3 can be a significant factor in later reading success. This is usually a book that children request over and over again and often attempt to 'read' for themselves, to their toys, brothers and sisters, or pets!

Learning that words are different from pictures

A big step towards reading is an understanding that words are different from pictures.

At first your toddler will simply see the words as black patterns on the page. But she will probably soon sense that they are important to you and will be curious about them. This is the best time to focus on the line of words and to explain that they tell you what to say– the words tell the story. You could also explain that one day, when your toddler can read, they will tell *her* the story, too.

You can draw attention to the words whenever you like. Your toddler will not be able to read them at this stage. She will make sense of them later. She might like to help you to point to the words as you go along. But don't try to make her. She'll enjoy remembering and saying some of them with you. Please don't insist that she's accurate–it isn't important.

Sound and picture games

Games like these develop children's looking and listening in pre-reading.

What's that? Hold your toddler's hand. Tell her to shut her eyes (it doesn't matter if she peeps) and ask her what she hears. Rustle a cornflake packet or hold a ticking clock close to her ear.

Which picture? When you've read a story, encourage your toddler to choose her 'best picture' in the book and to tell you about it. Who is in the picture? What's happening?

Silly word play Try making up rhyming lists–*moo, coo, blue, shoe. Silly Billy, Frilly Tilly*. It doesn't matter if they are nonsense–in fact, the more fun the better for learning.

Preparing your child to learn to read

Children will develop gradually and at their own pace towards successful reading. But your support during pre-reading will help to foster:

- positive attitudes towards books and reading.
- happy experiences of stories and rhymes.
- an understanding of how books work.
- some specific pre-reading skills.

Valuable pre-reading skills

Retelling – remembering and saying what happens in a story.

Sequencing – putting pictures and events in the right order.

Predicting – saying what will or might happen next.

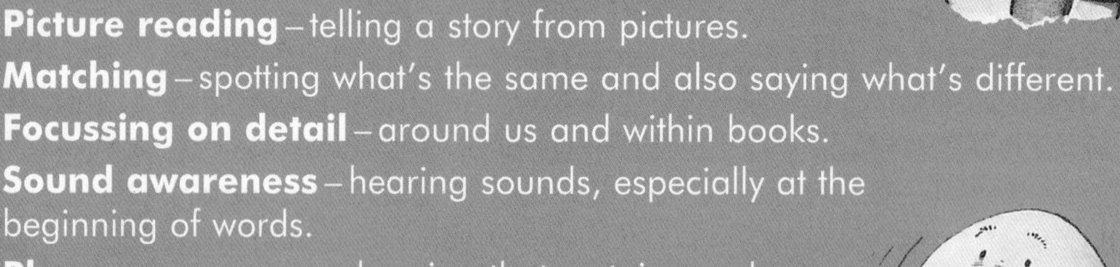

Picture reading – telling a story from pictures.

Matching – spotting what's the same and also saying what's different.

Focussing on detail – around us and within books.

Sound awareness – hearing sounds, especially at the beginning of words.

Rhyme awareness – hearing that certain words rhyme.

Rhyme memory – remembering nursery rhymes, songs and simple rhyming (or repetitive) stories.

Knowing letter names and letter sounds – beginning phonic knowledge.

Being able to read her name – and a few other words.

Environmental print

Print is all around us and children will begin to notice it almost automatically. But you can help to show that print is an important kind of pattern by pointing out what the words say on wrappers, tins, shop signs, and so on.

Being able to read print in the environment may not necessarily transfer to the print in books. This is because the word on a wrapper is associated with a distinctive colour and design.

The important point, though, is to encourage your child to recognise written detail around her.

Making sense of print in books

It's difficult to know exactly how children shift their attention to print as something distinct from patterns or detail in a picture. We can't see things in the same way that they do – and we're unlikely to be able to recall how we first came to look at words. But there are some useful things to remember at this stage.

- Continue to point to the words as you read, and encourage your child to do this with you.
- The shape of a word can help it to stay in the memory and be a clue to what it says the next time. It's useful if most of the words children see are in small letters (lower case). A word written entirely in capitals doesn't have such a distinctive shape.

- Exciting stories encourage children to want to make sense of print – so they can know for themselves what the words say.

The importance of memory

Learning to read depends on visual and auditory memory – sight and hearing. Memory holds the key role in reading and all other learning.

- Children will need to remember letter shapes and sounds, whole words and their meaning.
- Enjoyable repetition is vital for words to be stored in the memory. Rhymes and repetitive stories can help.
- Anxiety hinders the efficient use of memory, especially in early reading. Keep storytimes lighthearted and fun.
- Children usually remember those things that interest them – and are more likely to remember things that feel important to their world. Capture this interest with exciting stories that reflect their developing preferences.
- Enjoyable practice develops the memory. Games are great for this!

Memory and concentration games

These will encourage your child to enjoy looking and remembering. You take a turn, too.

Today I saw... When you come home from a shopping trip, can your child remember 5 things she saw? 10 things?

I packed my backpack and in it I put... *pencils, a teddy, a pair of red boots...* Take it in turns to remember the list and add to it.

I had a funny pet and it said... *hiccup, eeaw, moo...* Again, take turns to remember and add. This is a great one for parties.

I spy with my magic eye... Look closely together at a leaf, a flower, a wall. What detail or pattern can you see that you've never noticed before?

Spot the difference games are great for concentration and memory, too. Practise with the pages below.

The importance of rhyme

Hearing and seeing rhyme is very important for children's reading and for spelling later on. What matters most now is a positive attitude towards rhymes – the realisation that remembering rhyming stories and songs is great fun and that lots of important people in the family and at playgroup or nursery know nursery rhymes, too!

Have fun listing rhyming words, for example, *bat, sat, splat,* or take turns like a quiz.

Does elephant rhyme with cat?
Does dog rhyme with cat?
Does bat rhyme with cat?

Funny jingles and sentences that begin with the same letter are great for reinforcing sounds. For example, *happy hyenas have horrible howls*. It's even better if they rhyme.

When you talk about rhyming words, sometimes break them down into the beginning and end sounds when you pronounce them. Research has found that this helps children to learn how rhyme works and is useful for later reading.

f in fin

b in bin

Taken from Ladybird
Let's read together
First key words

Rhyme and reading

Researchers Bryant and Goswami have shown that children who can detect rhyme in English at 3-years old are more likely to experience reading success at age 6.

Letters and their sounds

At this stage, it's valuable to help your child to recognise and name the 26 letters of the alphabet and to be able to say the sounds made by the letters.

The letter **name** is **B** as in A**B**C.
The letter **sound** is how it sounds when spoken – **b**us.

Taken from Ladybird Get ready for reading *Alphabet songs*

Children need to know both letter names and sounds for reading, writing and spelling. Research shows that children benefit from activities that set out to teach and reinforce this alphabetic knowledge.

Fun with letter sounds and names

Talk about the names and sounds of the letters. What letter name and sound does your child's name begin with – and her friends' names?

Alphabet books are a great help here. These are books that introduce the letters and sounds of the alphabet. For this pre-reading stage, look for colourful and interesting alphabet books that offer more than simply the alphabet letters and an object. Look for detailed pictures, rhymes, games and funny phrases.

Go on a letter hunt! Look at food labels or book covers and see how many, say, **s** letters you can find.

Don't worry too much about alphabetical order at this stage, but you could try to sing the alphabet like a song! Have an alphabet chart in front of you and sing the letter names to the tune of a nursery rhyme, such as, *Twinkle, twinkle little star*.

Q What about letters that have more than one sound? (apple and ape; giant and goat)

A This is nothing to be worried about. If your child notices, then explain that, sometimes, letters can say different sounds.

Other ways to help your pre-reader

There is a large choice of material available to support your pre-reader at home. Add extra variety with:

Flashcards Typically, these are robust sets of cards that aim to boost letter-sound or word recognition. Children like handling and playing with these. It's best to avoid any activity that feels like a test of their ability to read the words. Look for colourful cards with lively illustrations to link the alphabet letter and sound, and that help you to play rhyming pairs, alphabet snap and other games.

Audio cassettes These offer traditional rhymes and humorous ways to introduce children to letters and sounds. Look for audio versions of children's stories, too.

Comics These are great if they are part of a more varied diet of stories, rhymes and pre-school activities.

TV and video Children can learn from their special children's programmes. TV and video are especially valuable for encouraging an appetite for stories and rhymes and an interest in particular characters. It is often helpful if you sit with your child and watch the programmes with her and talk about what you have seen. TV and videos shouldn't be regarded as a substitute for books, discussion and play.

What about writing?

It's great if learning to write develops alongside learning to read. Encouraging young children to take an interest in writing helps them to understand:

- that writing and print are important.
- the link between the written letters and the sounds they make when read.

Writing skills and stamina develop slowly. Give your child lots of opportunities to practise the kind of arm and hand movements needed for writing.

Many letters of the alphabet have similar shapes, and it's best to teach letter formation in these groups.

l t i y u

c o a d g q e

r n m h k b p

f j v w s x z

Helping beginner writers

Drawing, painting, crayoning, cutting and sticking all encourage hand/eye coordination and stamina. Let your child experiment with different sizes and types of pens, brushes and crayons, and on different writing surfaces.

Write any words your child requests in lower case (small) letters. (Use capitals only for the first letter of a name.) She may like you to put your hand gently over hers as she traces, so that you can help her with the writing movements.

Trace the formation of individual letters in the air and encourage your child to do this with you.

Make sure your child sees you writing – letters, lists, diaries.

If she shows a preference for writing with her left hand, don't discourage her. Children need encouragement for whichever hand they use more naturally.

Beginner writers need lots of praise for their efforts and to be made to feel their writing is important. Display the results!

"A letter."
Katy (age 2)

"To Grandma,
We've been to Tesco's."
Catherine (age 3)

"To Daddy,
I am going to wear something what lives at castles when I get home."
Michael (age 4)

What are the most important things to remember?

- Reading a variety of illustrated stories and rhymes to and with your child is the happiest and most powerful way to stimulate her to want to learn to read.
- Help her to learn letter names and to hear the sounds that the letters make.

First choice for

Get ready for reading

A comprehensive collection to equip your child with valuable pre-reading skills (see page 18).

Let's read together

Traditional stories and new rhymes to build the confidence and skills of children who have just started reading.

First steps

A series of 10 books, with flashcards, to develop early learning concepts.

pre-reading

Favourite tales

Picture Ladybirds

9312*

S9524*

Storytime

SL1

946*

S808*
S9544*

*Other titles and book and tape packs available

Reading (4½–7 years)

What's happening now?

A tremendous amount! Your child will be starting school. He'll be finding out about maths, science, technology, history and geography, and gaining other knowledge and skills he can use throughout his adult life. He'll probably be learning to swim and to ride a bike. Most important of all, of course, he'll be learning to read.

From pre-reading to reading

The transition from pre-reading to real reading is almost imperceptible. Reading researcher Henry Pearson describes this sequence of learning as moving *'from playing at reading, to reciting text, to recognising words in the text, to reading the text'*.

There is no standard age at which all children are ready, physically and emotionally, to begin to read – but there is an optimum state known by educationalists as *'readiness for reading'*. This is not a mysterious idea if you accept that some children are ready to begin learning to read earlier than others. Reading readiness takes account of your child's language, coordination, play, concentration and curiosity about stories and the written word. If all these factors are well developed in your pre-school child and he is happy to spend a few minutes each day trying to learn to read, then by all means see what you can do together.

Reading readiness checklist

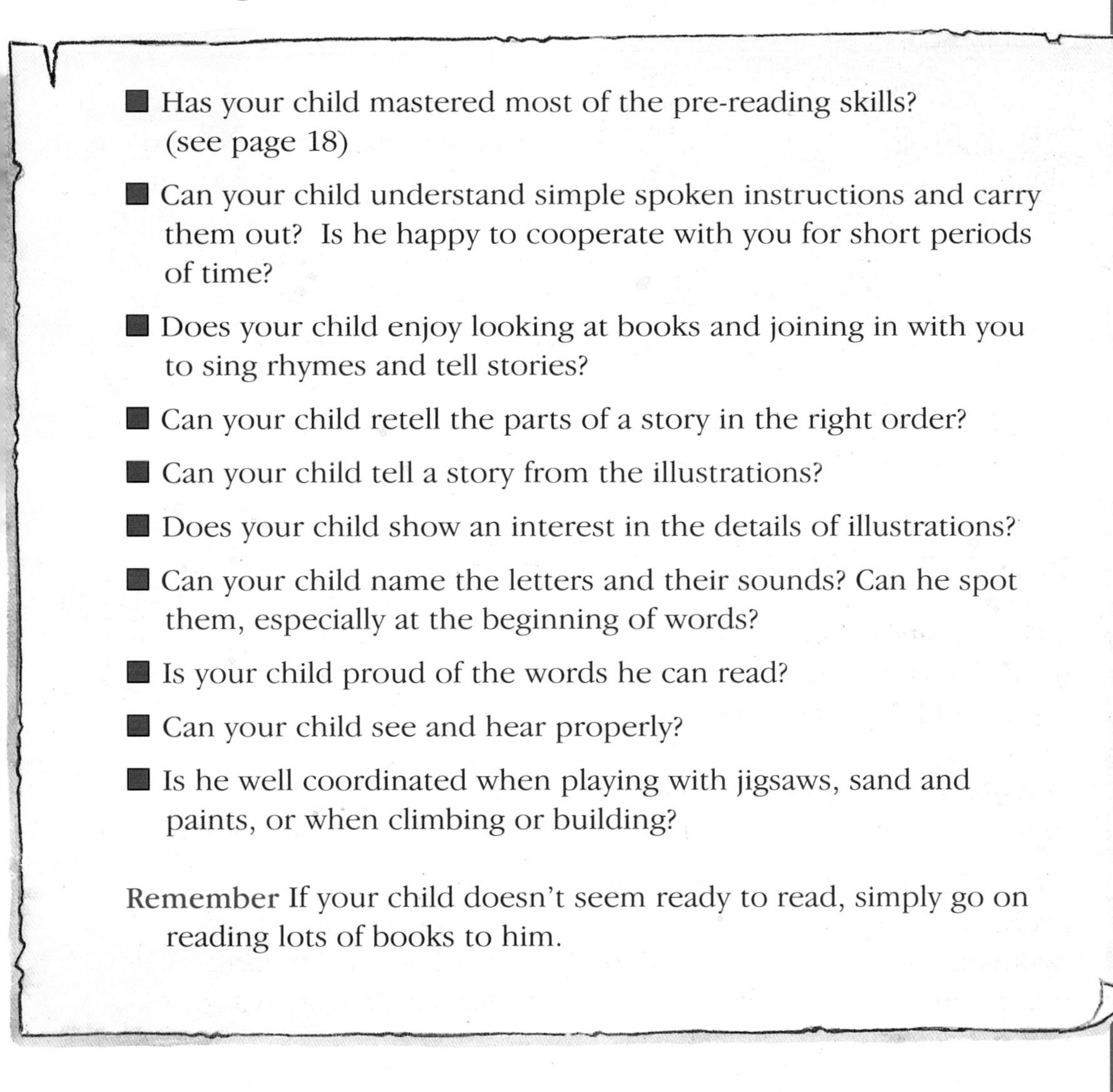

- Has your child mastered most of the pre-reading skills? (see page 18)
- Can your child understand simple spoken instructions and carry them out? Is he happy to cooperate with you for short periods of time?
- Does your child enjoy looking at books and joining in with you to sing rhymes and tell stories?
- Can your child retell the parts of a story in the right order?
- Can your child tell a story from the illustrations?
- Does your child show an interest in the details of illustrations?
- Can your child name the letters and their sounds? Can he spot them, especially at the beginning of words?
- Is your child proud of the words he can read?
- Can your child see and hear properly?
- Is he well coordinated when playing with jigsaws, sand and paints, or when climbing or building?

Remember If your child doesn't seem ready to read, simply go on reading lots of books to him.

At this point you could help your child by choosing a simple structured reading programme, such as *Read with Ladybird*. This type of material will be equally beneficial as reading support once your child has started school.

Why reading support at home is so valuable once your child is at school

Your encouragement at home continues to be very important at all stages in reading – even when your child can read for himself.

- Short sessions of reading with you, one-to-one, will give him valuable practice and establish a firm foundation.
- When home and school work together in partnership, it gives children a lovely feeling of security.
- Struggling readers can benefit especially from informed home support.

Getting involved

Often parents are unsure exactly what to do and feel guilty because they frequently have little time available to read with their children. But here are two things that you might consider.

Ask your child's teacher for advice. Tell her that you have, say, 10 minutes each day for helping your child with his reading and ask what's the best thing for you to do. Then keep in touch on how you are progressing.

Use this Guide to give you insight into the most effective and happiest ways to support your child as he learns to read.

Offer encouragement

We can encourage in so many ways – through what we say and write, through body language, hugs, applause! Used effectively, encouragement gives hope and a sense of significance. It stimulates physical and mental energy and creates an atmosphere in which children want to master new steps.

Encouragement gives courage!

Handy hints for helping

- Find a suitable time for reading – when your child isn't tired, hungry or absorbed in something else.

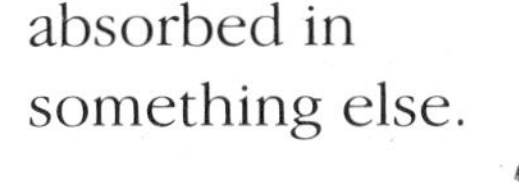

- Choose short books and stories so your child doesn't feel daunted by the length of them!

- Keep reading sessions short – 10 minutes a day or several times a week is fine. Always end on a happy note – don't press on until you both get tired.

- Look for stories you know will interest him and ask his opinion on the stories and the characters in them.

- Look for funny stories so you can enjoy a good laugh together.

- Specific praise is very powerful: *'You read the way they speak really well.' 'I love the way you read that rhyme, it made me laugh.'*

- Re-read familiar stories together – stories your child can enjoy reading fluently.

- Tell your child how much you enjoy reading with him.

- Keep up the bedtime stories!

Q What should I do when my child gets a word wrong?

A It's often best simply to give the right word and let your child carry on. Mistakes are useful clues to how children try to work out words.

Ask yourself: Is the story predictable enough? Would more talking about what's happening help? Would more general focus on letters and sounds help him to work out the first letter of the word he doesn't know?

How is reading taught in schools?

A number of approaches are adopted in schools and you will sometimes hear about them in media reports. Teachers usually don't select a single method, but combine the various approaches.

Hopefully, your child will be taught to read in the way that most suits the way he learns.

Different methods explained

The **phonic** method aims to build up an understanding of how our alphabetic system works – of the letters and the sounds they represent. This knowledge helps children to tackle words they don't know.

Look-and-say aims to teach children a growing sight vocabulary of complete words that they can recognise and read at once. The method relies upon high rates of repetition of these words within the book or story. This approach is usually at the heart of reading programmes that have a controlled vocabulary.

The **'real' books/whole language** approach aims to absorb children's attention so much in exciting stories and natural language that they will begin to focus on, predict and remember the words they see. The stories selected are not usually from schemes specifically designed to teach reading.

These days, most schools actively encourage our help, often sending books home to read together and holding parents' events to explain the school's reading methods. Some schools ask parents to help by **shared reading**. This is simply a way of reading books to and with your child, and encouraging him to read more and more of the words for himself. The notes in this Guide will help you. **Paired reading** is a more patterned approach. You and your child read aloud together until your child tells you (by an agreed signal – such as tapping you on the hand) that he's ready to read by himself. You then let him carry on alone. When he comes to a word he cannot read or work out, you tell him the word and carry on reading aloud together until he signals to you again.

How the approaches can be combined

Fancy dress zoo is a story from the *Read with Ladybird* range. It is a good example of an entertaining, amusing story that has been specially written to help young children to learn to read, using a combination of the phonic, look-and-say or whole language methods.

- The pictures provide useful clues to the words.
- Phrases are repeated to reinforce learning and to help your child predict the text.
- Many of the words, for example, *we, a, had, and, the,* are key words (see page 35) – important words that should form the basis of a child's sight vocabulary.
- Natural language, *We had a really good party*, helps children to predict some of the words.

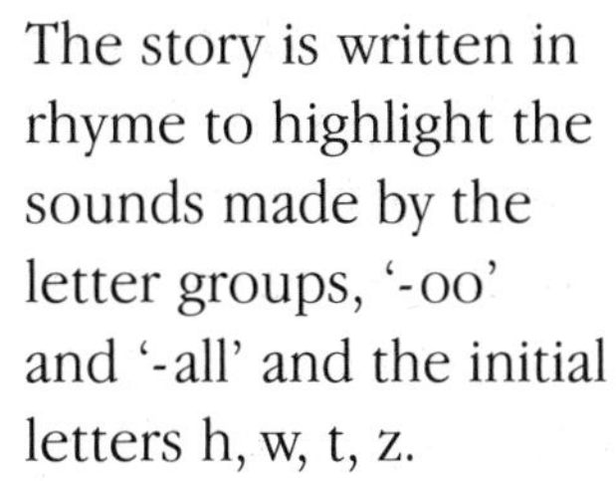

- The story is written in rhyme to highlight the sounds made by the letter groups, '-oo' and '-all' and the initial letters h, w, t, z.

On becoming a real reader

As your child understands how books and stories work and uses his pre-reading skills, he will start to get meaning from some of the print for himself. This ability will develop and improve as he learns various ways or *strategies* to help him to get more meaning from the print. He will then need to practise to reinforce and encourage his new-found skills on the road to independent reading. The kind of support you give will vary according to your child's changing needs. He may also have ideas about the kind of help he wants, and it's great to enlist your child's opinions as to how he learns best!

Reading strategies explained

Reading skills can be isolated and explained separately for clarification. But it's important to realise that they work together, with some being more dominant at certain stages. The following are some of the most effective strategies children use in learning to read.

Memory – remembering details of the story, sentences and individual words.

Picture 'cues' – looking at the story told by the pictures is a vital strategy that starts in pre-reading. When actual reading begins, children use the pictures and the words together to understand the story. As reading progresses the illustrations gradually become part of the overall enjoyment of the book and function less as a direct tool for reading.

Context clues – guessing what the word is likely to be from what is happening in the story.

Prediction – trying to predict what the word will be from their developing knowledge of the structure and grammar of our language – what word is likely to come next.

Phonic awareness – becoming increasingly aware of recurring patterns of letters and sounds. Children may first look at the initial letter of a word and say its sound. Later they may also concentrate on the letter sounds within and at the ends of words.

A developing sight vocabulary – memorising more and more key words, as reading progresses. This also helps children to focus on other new words.

Making sense – children know that the story needs to make sense and will often guess a word from clues in the context – and from their knowledge of our speech patterns. This is a very valuable strategy – especially in conjunction with phonic and letter pattern clues. Children will begin to realise when they have made a mistake – and will want to correct it.

Using punctuation – developing an understanding of how the punctuation marks contribute to the meaning of what they are reading.

Key words

These are the words used most frequently in the English language. Research shows that 100 of these words form half the total number of words found in children's reading material. (Murray and McNally, 1962)
Although these words occur so frequently, they can be tricky to learn because they are difficult to illustrate, for example, *he, she, here, this, where*. Help your child to learn them by choosing some stories that are designed to repeat these vital words. Ask your child's teacher or use the guidance notes inside reading books.

Start reading

When your child starts to read aloud, he will be relying on your help and encouragement.

How to help your starting reader

First read the story to your child before he reads it to you and make opportunities to read it again. If there are any repeated sentences in the story, have fun reading these together like the chorus in a song. **Talk about the pictures.** You could look at all the pictures first, then go back and read the words. Don't cover up the pictures to prove your child can read. **Encourage informed guesses.** Prompt gently by asking what he thinks the word could be. What letter-sound does it start with? **Read lots of rhyming stories together**.

Choosing books to support starting readers

- Choose simple, entertaining stories with lively illustrations.
- Choose short rhyming stories that your child can memorise.
- Look for interesting activity books that encourage your child to enjoy and practise writing.

Avoid pressure

One concern about home support is that children could feel under pressure – that our love depends on whether or not they can read the next word. Or they could feel that they are being compared unfavourably with friends or siblings. Pressure causes anxiety and this can adversely affect memory and reading.
Pressure usually arises because we are concerned that our children should do well. We can channel this concern into effective encouragement instead! (See page 30.)

The National Curriculum: Reading at Key Stage 1

The National Curriculum Orders (1995) Programmes of Study for Reading state that 'Pupils should be given extensive experience of children's literature,' and that this experience should include stories, poetry, picture books, plays and children's own written material. The requirements for Key Skills at this Stage emphasise the need for understanding and enjoyment in learning to read. They require that children should be taught to use 'various approaches to word identification and recognition, and to use their understanding of grammatical structure and the meaning of the text as a whole to make sense of print'.

I'm happy.

I'm sad.

28

Taken from
Read with Ladybird
Level 1, book 4
Stuck in the mud

Talking about punctuation

Understanding punctuation helps children with the meaning of what they read. These simplified explanations may help.

! An exclamation mark means that we say the word or sentence with lots of feeling.

. A full stop shows it's the end of the sentence and we need to pause for breath. Remember there's a capital letter at the beginning of each sentence.

, A comma tells us we need a little pause.

? A question mark tells us that a question is being asked.

' An apostrophe tells us that a letter is being left out or that something belongs to someone.

“” Double or **‘’** single speech marks go round what's being said.

Improve reading

This stage is one of increased concentration on the story told by the words themselves, as well as by the words and pictures working together. You will both be experiencing the lovely feeling that *'He's really reading!'*

The improving reader will be: relying on your help but attempting more himself; reading aloud slowly as he uses his reading strategies to work out new words; enjoying reading fluency as he reads familiar sentences with a more natural speed; and developing stamina in reading slightly longer stories. He will still need encouragement and praise to acknowledge his efforts!

How to help your improving reader

Continue to offer to read the story to him first. (He may not want this now, but ask anyway.) Be happy to **hear the stories again**. Continue to **show interest in the pictures**. Always appear pleased to **help with a word your child cannot read**. Encourage the use of phonic knowledge (especially with words he cannot read), guessing and self-correction. **Read the whole sentence again** after you've talked about a mistake. **Explain punctuation**, if your child asks, and read the words in speech marks in lively ways!

Taken from
Read with Ladybird
Level 2, book 6
A quiet night out

I wish I could run faster.
I wish I could climb a tree.
I wish I could be lots of things.
But I'm really glad I'm **me!**

32

Choosing books to support the improving reader

Variety matters! Choose:

- short, entertaining first reading material – but be a little more adventurous now.
- stories, rhymes and poems that have interesting and rewarding words.
- stories that accurately reflect your child's world.
- interesting fact books. Some early readers prefer these to storybooks.
- lively activity books that encourage reading and writing.

Practise reading

This is an exciting, hard-working stage – children need to practise reading as they move towards becoming independent readers.

At this stage, the young reader will: be in need of your unobtrusive help (and may resent it, if you jump in to help too quickly); often be enjoying reading silently; be selecting from a range of strategies to work out new words; be becoming a faster reader (although he may sound quite slow if he reads aloud); be increasing his reading stamina; and be forming strong opinions about the kinds of books he likes.

If reading has been successful, he will begin to realise that the world of reading is open to him and be willing to make the effort to reach it.

He will also be enjoying pictures but not relying on them to give the meaning of words. Non-fiction and information books are an exception to this, as detailed pictures may carry meaning to technical words.

Choosing books to support your practising reader

- Look for books that offer simple tasters of the wider world of reading – strong stories, fables, poetry, rhymes, puzzles and information books.
- Encourage your child to choose his own books and give him lots of support to read them.

Q What are the most important things to remember?

A Respect your child's choice of books (Try not to say '*Not football/horses again...*') and be ready to talk about them.

- Be gently supportive when your child reads aloud to you. Don't react quickly to mistakes. Give him a chance to correct himself before offering to help.
- Understand when your child prefers simpler, younger books. We often read to relax, and it's important that not all reading material is challenging.
- Carry on reading to your child and discuss the enjoyment you get from books.

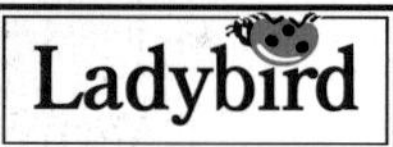

First choice for

Read with Ladybird

A simple, structured reading programme that combines the different approaches to teaching that are used in schools (see page 32).

Level 1 – Start reading

- simple, entertaining stories with lively illustrations
- short rhyming stories for your child to remember
- careful introduction of the most frequently used words

Level 2 – Improve reading

- stories and rhymes with interesting and rewarding words
- encourages the use and development of reading strategies (see pages 34 and 35)
- builds on a bank of familiar words to encourage confidence
- pages of interesting facts to add an extra dimension to stories

Level 3 – Practise reading

- increases reading stamina
- wide range of different stories
- books your child would choose for himself

S9719

reading

Read it yourself

A selection of traditional tales your child can read to you.

9317

Read with me

A look-and-say approach to learning to read, introducing 300 of the most frequently used words in the English language. Includes 16 readers, 6 activity books, picture word cards and audio cassettes.

9325

S9328

S9326

Say the Sounds

A phonics reading scheme that includes 8 readers, 4 activity books, flash cards and double audio cassette.

9310

CSS/1

S9315

S9311

Reluctant readers

When should children be reading?

Most educationalists agree that we would expect to see some signs of reading after 3 terms at school. Children really do progress at different rates so it's hard to say exactly what progress should have been made. Most of us would hope that our children had made reasonable progress in reading by the age of 7.

How you can help a reluctant reader

Start by getting all the information you can about the best ways to encourage reading. This Guide will help.

Remember that most reading theory (including this Guide) presupposes a cooperative child – and when children refuse to concentrate or tell us they don't like reading we can feel failures ourselves. We can feel that other parents are obviously able to make better relationships with their children.

We need to find ways to dispel these anxious feelings before we look at the actual mechanics of reading.

What matters most is to re-establish books as a source of fun and enjoyment – not as things to test your child.

Talk it over...

Try to let your child's interests lead you, and resist the temptation to take over and perhaps push too hard. Talk with him about ways to help. Even at this young age, it's important that children have an active interest in how they learn. In a relaxed and happy atmosphere, children often give you valuable insights into their feelings and put forward excellent ideas for learning. Show your pride in him and what he achieves.

Other points to consider

- Check with your child's teacher. Explain that you understand how important it is not to show anxiety or apply pressure.
- Read lots more stories to your child without asking him to read anything to you.
- Can he recognise letters? Does he know the sounds they make?
- Encourage him to choose his own books. Explain that he doesn't have to choose books he can read – you will read the books to him!
- How does your child like to learn? Does he want you to read the story or sentence first – or would he like you both to read it together? The paired reading method (see page 32) can be especially supportive for struggling readers.
- Are there any information books or magazines that would interest him? Showing how much we value their interests is often an effective way to bring children back to books.
- Computer games can be a rival to reading. Be positive about children's interest in computers. Praise their expertise. Don't make them feel they have to choose between computers and books.
- Look for books that are funny. Laughing over a book is one of the happiest ways to help children to concentrate and improve.
- It would be wise to have your child's hearing and sight tested.

Q My child is struggling with reading. Does that mean that he is dyslexic?

A Dyslexia is the name given to a specific learning difficulty that usually affects children's reading, writing, spelling, maths, memory and organisational skills. Dyslexic children often benefit from a structured, systematic teaching approach.

Check with your child's teacher and ask how the school can help him. For further information contact:

British Dyslexia Association
98 London Road
Reading Berks RG1 5AU

The Dyslexia Institute
133 Gresham Road
Staines Middlesex TW18 2AJ

The wider world of reading (7+)

What's happening now?

The 7-year old is leaving early childhood behind, gaining in confidence and personality. She's maturing in understanding of life's experiences, and these are now becoming more those of the adult world with an emphasis on status and current fashion. It's a time of opportunity and for encouraging early talent in music, sport and dancing. The 7-year old needs the loving security of her home – but she's also preoccupied with what her friends are saying, doing, wearing.

Getting hooked on books

What matters now is that children want to read and see the point of making this big effort. Motivation is everything!

At this stage, young readers will: usually read silently; vary considerably in their fluency and reading stamina; be forming a lasting opinion as to whether reading is for them or not; be aware of the differences between their reading success and that of their classmates; be in need of our interest and pride and encouraged by feeling we are still happy to help.

Choosing books to support the 7+ reader

Help to broaden the reading adventure by encouraging your child to choose from a wide variety of books. It's the appetite for reading that counts, and it's best to avoid judgments about whether one kind of book is better than another. Most of us enjoy some books that stretch us – and others that help us to unwind.

Widening the world of reading

Children vary in their reading tastes. So it's rewarding for them to choose from a wide variety of books and stories. Make time to browse in bookshops.

Look for reviews of children's books in newspapers and magazines. Read them with your child. Is it worth tracking the book down?

Encourage your child to look for and re-read stories she has enjoyed reading or hearing at school.

Information books are becoming increasingly sophisticated and interactive. Enjoy these with your child.

Electronic books

The cultural choices open to our children are almost limitless, and books are becoming one part of a fast-developing range of information and entertainment. Children's reading and information skills are now widely supported by audio and computer sources, CD ROM and the Internet. Efficient use of electronic books is boosted by being a fast, accurate reader.

The National Curriculum

Reading at Key Stage 2

The National Curriculum Orders for English (1995) at Key Stage 2 emphasise that 'Pupils should be encouraged to develop as enthusiastic, independent and reflective readers. They should be introduced to a wide range of literature, and have opportunities to read extensively for their own interest and pleasure, and for information'. Children's reading can be developed by offering them 'progressively more challenging and demanding texts'.

The Classics

Classics are well-established contemporary children's stories (for example, *Tarka the Otter, Fantastic Mr Fox, Goodnight Mister Tom*) and adult stories (*Treasure Island, Wind in the Willows*) that have stood the test of time. Simplified versions of the classics are valuable for capturing a child's enjoyment of the famous plots before she has developed the stamina and skill to tackle the actual text.

What are the most important ways to help at 7+?

- Provide opportunities for your child to read – quiet times and a suitable place – maybe a corner or a den for reading.
- Ask your child's opinion as to whether you would enjoy one of her books – and act on her recommendations.
- Make sure she can find her way around information books – that she can use the contents list and the index, understands roman numerals and knows how encyclopedias work.
- Go on encouraging your child to read lively and exciting stories, and show how much you enjoy reading to find out what's going to happen next, too.
- Look for books that relate to stories shown or serialised on TV or made into films, so that your child will be familiar with the plot and realise how entertaining the story is. Simplified classics are great, as they concentrate on the elements that children most enjoy – what happens and the people it's happening to!
- Make opportunities for 'real' and important writing activities… lists, diaries, games.

Don't stop reading to and with your 7+ child if she would like to read with you!

AND THE MOST IMPORTANT MESSAGE OF ALL IS – ENJOY BOOKS!

Ladybird – First choice for 7+

Classic tales

Simplified versions of well-established, popular stories.

9420†*

SL1

954*

955*

*Other titles and book and tape packs available

Reading for information

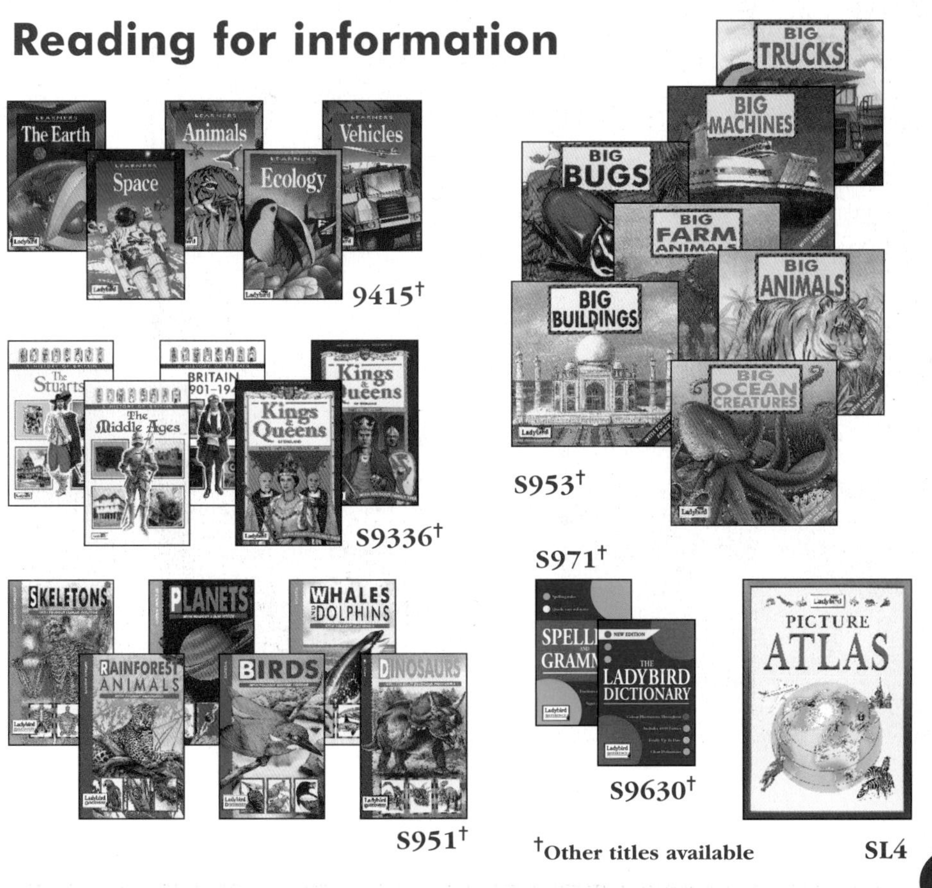

9415†

S953†

S9336†

S971†

S9630†

S951†

SL4

†Other titles available

Index